CONTENTS

 2
 3
 4
 8
 10
 12
 14
 16
 18
 20
 22
 23
 24

For pattern inquiries, please visit: www.go-crafty.com

CROCHET HAPPY BABY BLANKET

YARN
Bernat® Baby Sport™ (12.3 oz/ 350 g; 1256 yds/1148 m)
Baby Green (21230) 2 balls

HOOK
Size U.S. G/6 (4 mm) crochet hook *or size needed to obtain gauge.*

LEARN BY VIDEO
www.go-crafty.com
Ch (chain)
Dc (double crochet)
Sc (single crochet)

MEASUREMENT
Approx 40½" [105.5 cm] square.

GAUGE
16 dc and 8 rows = 4" [10 cm].

INSTRUCTIONS
Ch 160.
1st row: (RS). 1 dc in 4th ch from hook. 1 dc in each ch to end of chain. Turn. 158 dc.
2nd row: Ch 3 (counts as dc). 1 dc in next dc. *Ch 2. Skip next 2 dc. 1 dc in each of next 2 dc. Rep from * to end of row. Turn.
3rd row: Ch 3 (counts as dc). 1 dc in next dc. 2 dc in next ch-2 sp. *1 dc in each of next 2 dc. 2 dc in next ch-2 sp. Rep from * to last 2 dc. 1 dc in each of last 2 dc. Turn.
4th row: Ch 4 (counts at dc and ch 1). Skip next dc. 1 dc in each of next 2 dc. *Ch 2. Skip next 2 dc. 1 dc in each of next 2 dc. Rep from * to last 2 dc. Ch 1. Skip next dc. 1 dc in last dc. Turn.
5th row: Ch 3 (counts as dc). 1 dc in next ch-1 sp. 1 dc in each of next 2 dc. *2 dc in next ch-2 sp. 1 dc in each of next 2 dc. Rep from * to last 2 sts. 1 dc in 4th and 3rd ch of beg ch-4. Turn.
Rep 2nd to 5th rows for pat until Blanket measures approx 39" [99 cm] from beg, ending on a 3rd or 5th row of pat.
Fasten off.

FINISHING
Edging: 1st rnd: (RS). Join yarn with sl st to any corner of Blanket. Ch 1. Work 1 rnd of sc evenly around Blanket, having 3 sc in corners. Join with sl st to first sc.
2nd and 3rd rnds: Ch 1. 1 sc in each sc around, having 3 sc in corner sc. Join with sl st to first sc.
Fasten off. ■

COLORBLOCK CROCHET BLANKET

YARN
Bernat® Baby Blanket™
(3.5 oz/100 g; 72 yds/65 m)
Contrast A Vanilla (03008)
2 balls or 142 yds/130 m
Contrast B Baby Sand (03010)
2 balls or 142 yds/130 m
Contrast C Baby Teal (03734)
2 balls or 142 yds/130 m
Contrast D Seafoam (03736)
2 balls or 142 yds/130 m

HOOK
Size U.S. J/10 (6 mm)
crochet hook *or size needed
to obtain gauge.*

LEARN BY VIDEO
www.go-crafty.com
Ch (chain)
Sc (single crochet)

MEASUREMENTS
Approx 36" by 40" [91 x 101 cm].

GAUGE
7 sc and 8 rows = 4" [10 cm].

INSTRUCTIONS
With A, chain (ch) 64.
1st row: [Right Side (RS)]. 1 single crochet (sc) in 2nd ch from hook. 1 sc in each ch to end of chain. Turn. 63 sc.
2nd row: Ch 1. 1 sc in each sc to end of row. Turn.
Repeat (Rep) 2nd row until work from beginning (beg) measures 10" [25.5 cm], ending on a Wrong Side (WS) row.
With B, rep 2nd row until work from beg measures 20" [51 cm], ending on a WS row.
With C, rep 2nd row until work from beg measures 30" [76 cm], ending on a WS row.
With D, rep 2nd row until work from beg measures 40" [101.5 cm], ending on a WS row. Fasten off. ∎

COZY CROCHET HOODIE

YARN
Bernat® Softee® Baby™
(5 oz/140 g; 362 yds /331 m)
Sizes 6 (12-18-24) mos: Flannel
(30044) 2 (2-3-3) balls

HOOK
Sizes U.S. G/6 (4 mm) crochet hook *or size needed to obtain gauge.*

ADDITIONAL
Stitch markers
4 buttons

LEARN BY VIDEO
www.go-crafty.com
Ch (chain)
Sc (single crochet)
Dc (double crochet)
Slip stitch
Hdc2tog (half double crochet 2 stitches together)

SIZES
To fit chest measurement
6 mos 17" [43 cm]
12 mos 18" [45.5 cm]
18 mos 19" [48.5 cm]
24 mos 20" [51 cm]

Finished chest
6 mos 20" [51 cm]
12 mos 21" [53 cm]
18 mos 22" [56 cm]
24 mos 23" [58.5 cm]

GAUGE
16 sts and 12 rows = 4" [10 cm] in pat.

INSTRUCTIONS
The instructions are written for smallest size. If changes are necessary for larger sizes the instructions will be written thus ( ). When only one number is given, it applies to all sizes.

BACK
Ch 42 (44-46-48).
1st row: (RS). 1 sc in 2nd ch from hook. *1 dc in next ch. 1 sc in next ch. Rep from * to end of chain. Turn. 41 (43-45-47) sts.
2nd row: Ch 3 (counts as dc). *1 sc in next dc. 1 dc in next sc. Rep from * to end of row. Turn.
3rd row: Ch 1. 1 sc in first dc. *1 dc in next sc. 1 sc in next dc. Rep from * to end of row. Turn.
Rep last 2 rows for pat until work from beg measures 7 (7½-8-8½)" [18 (19-20.5-21.5) cm], ending on a WS row.

Shape armholes: Next row: (RS). Sl st across first 3 sts. Ch 1. 1 sc in same sp as last sl st. Pat to last 2 sts. Turn. Leave rem 2 sts unworked.
Cont even in pat over rem 37 (39-41-43) sts until armhole measures 4 (4½-4½-5)" [10 (11.5-11.5-12.5) cm], ending on a WS row.
Fasten off.

RIGHT FRONT
**Ch 32 (34-36-38).
1st row: (RS). 1 sc in 2nd ch from hook. *1 dc in next ch. 1 sc in next ch. Rep from * to end of chain. Turn. 31 (33-35-37) sts.
Cont in pat as given for Back until work from beg measures 7 (7½-8-8½)" [18 (19-20.5-21.5) cm], ending on a WS row.**

Shape armhole: Next row: (RS). Pat to last 2 sts. Turn. Leave rem sts unworked.
Cont even in pat over rem 29 (31-33-35) sts until armhole measures 6 rows less than Back, ending on a WS row. Fasten off.

Shape neck: 1st row: (RS). Skip first 13 (14-16-17) sts. Join yarn with sl st to next st. Ch 2 (does not count as st). Hdc2tog over same st as last sl st and next st. Pat to end of row. Turn.
2nd row: Pat to last 2 sts. Hdc2tog. Turn.
3rd row: Ch 2 (does not count as st). Hdc2tog. Pat to end of row. Turn.
Rep last 2 rows once more, then 2nd row once. 10 (11-11-12) sts. Fasten off.
Place markers for 4 buttons on Right Front in 2 rows (double breasted), spaced as follows: Top row of 2 buttons positioned 2 rows down from neck edge—first button 1" [2.5 cm] from front edge; second button 4" [10 cm] from front edge (3" [7.5 cm] apart from each other).
Bottom row of 2 buttons positioned 10 rows down from neck edge—first button 1" [2.5 cm] from front edge; second button 4" [10 cm] from front edge (3" [7.5 cm] apart from each other).

LEFT FRONT
Note: Work buttonhole row to correspond to markers on Right Front as follows:
Buttonhole row: (RS). (Pat to button marker. Ch 1. Skip next st) twice. Pat to end of row.
Work from ** to ** as given for Right Front.

COZY CROCHET HOODIE

SLEEVES

Ch 28 (30-30-34).

1st row: (RS). 1 sc in 2nd ch from hook. *1 dc in next ch. 1 sc in next ch. Rep from * to end of chain. Turn. 27 (29-29-33) sts.

Cont in pat as given for Back for 5 more rows.

Shape sides: 1st row: (RS-Inc row). Ch 3 (counts as dc). 1 sc in first dc. *1 dc in next sc. 1 sc in next dc. Rep from * to last 2 sts. 1 dc in next sc. (1 sc. 1 dc) in last dc. Turn.

2nd row: Ch 1. 1 sc in first dc. *1 dc in next sc. 1 sc in next dc. Rep from * to end of row. Turn.

3rd row: Ch 3 (counts as dc). *1 sc in next dc. 1 dc in next sc. Rep from * to end of row. Turn.

4th and 5th rows: As 2nd and 3rd rows.

Rep last 5 rows twice more. 33 (35-35-39) sts.

Cont even in pat until work from beg measures 7 (7½-8-8½)" [18 (19-20.5-21.5) cm], ending on a WS row. Place markers at each end of last row. Work 2 rows even in pat. Fasten off.

POCKETS

Ch 16 (16-18-18).

1st row: (RS). 1 sc in 2nd ch from hook. *1 dc in next ch. 1 sc in next ch. Rep from * to end of chain. Turn. 15 (15-17-17) sts.

Cont in pat as given for Back for 2 (2-2½-2½)" [5 (5-6.5-6.5) cm], ending on a WS row.

Shape sides: 1st row: (RS). Ch 2 (does not count as st). Hdc2tog. Pat to last 2 sts. Hdc2tog. Turn.

Rep last row twice more. 9 (9-11-11) sts. Fasten off.

Shape armhole: Next row: (RS). Sl st across first 3 sts. Ch 1. 1 sc in same sp as last sl st. Pat to end of row. Turn. Cont even in pat over rem 29 (31-33-35) sts until armhole measures 6 rows less than Back (working buttonhole row to correspond to markers on Right Front), ending on a WS row.

Shape neck: 1st row: (RS). Pat across 14 (15-15-16) sts. Hdc2tog (neck edge). Turn. Leave rem sts unworked.

2nd row: Ch 2 (does not count as st). Hdc2tog. Pat to end of row. Turn.

3rd row: Pat to last 2 sts. Hdc2tog. Turn.

4th row: As 2nd row.

5th row: Buttonhole row: (RS). (Pat to button marker. Ch 1. Skip next st) twice. Pat to last 2 sts. Hdctog. Turn.

6th row: As 2nd row. 10 (11-11-12) sts. Fasten off.

FINISHING

Sew shoulder seams. Sew in sleeves, placing rows above markers along unworked sts of Body to form square armholes. Sew side and sleeve seams, reversing seam for 1½" [4.5 cm] cuff turnback.

Hood: Place markers on neck edge 3" [7.5 cm] in from front edge.
With RS facing, join yarn with sl st at Right Front neck marker. Ch 1.
Work 71 (71-75-75) sc evenly around neck edge to opposite marker. Turn.

Next row: Ch 1. 1 sc in first sc. *1 dc in next sc. 1 sc in next sc. Rep from * end of row. Turn. Place marker on center back st.

Next row: (RS). Ch 3 (counts as dc). (1 sc in next dc. 1 dc in next sc) 17 (17-18-18) times. (1 sc. 1 dc. 1 sc) all in next dc (center back st). (1 dc in next sc. 1 sc in next dc) 17 (17-18-18) times. 1 dc in last sc. Turn.
Work 3 rows even in pat.

Next row: (RS). Ch 3 (counts as dc). (1 sc in next dc. 1 dc in next sc) 17 (17-18-18) times. 1 sc in next dc. (1 dc. 1 sc. 1 dc) all in next sc (center back st). (1 sc in next dc. 1 dc in next sc) 18 (18-19-19) times. Turn.
Work 3 rows even in pat.

Next row: (RS). Ch 3 (counts as dc). (1 sc in next dc. 1 dc in next sc) 18 (18-19-19) times. (1 sc. 1 dc. 1 sc) all in next dc (center back st). (1 dc in next sc. 1 sc in next dc) 18 (17-18-18) times. 1 dc in last sc. Turn. 77 (77-81-81) sts.
Cont even in pat until Hood measures 8 (8½-8½-9)" [20.5 (21.5-21.5-23) cm] from neck edge, ending on a WS row. Fasten off. Fold Hood in half and sew top Hood seam. Sew buttons and Pockets in position.

POMPOM

Wind yarn around 3 fingers approx. 100 times. Remove from fingers and tie tightly in center. Cut through each side of loops. Trim to a smooth round shape. Sew to end of Hood.

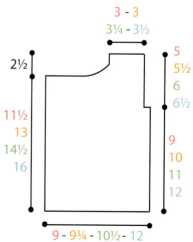
Pompom

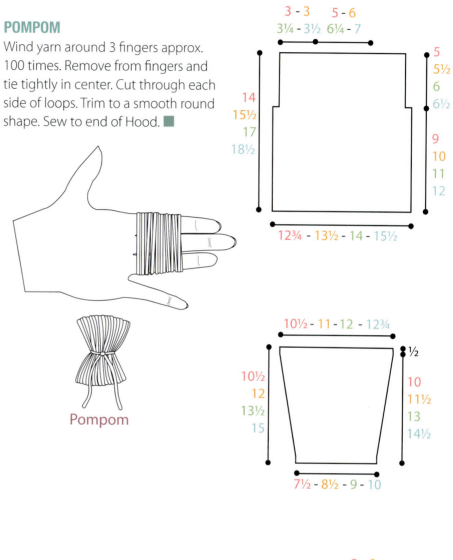

WEE CROCHET MOCCASINS

YARN
Bernat® Softee® Baby™ (5 oz/140 g; 362 yds/331 m)
Main Color (MC) Little Mouse (30010) 1 ball
Contrast A Aqua (30201) 1 ball
Contrast B Soft Red (30424) 1 ball

HOOK
Size U.S. G/6 (4 mm) crochet hook *or size needed to obtain gauge.*

ADDITIONAL
Stitch marker

LEARN BY VIDEO
www.go-crafty.com
Ch (chain)
Sc (single crochet)
Hdc (half double crochet)
Slip stitch
Sc2tog (single crochet 2 stitches together)
Pompom

SIZE
One size: To fit baby 3–6 months.

GAUGE
16 sc and 19 rows = 4" [10 cm].

INSTRUCTIONS
Foot: With MC, ch 9.
1st rnd: 1 sc in 2nd ch from hook. 1 sc in each of next 6 ch. 3 sc in last ch. Working into opposite side of ch, 1 sc in each of next 6 ch. 2 sc in last ch. Join with sl st to first sc. 18 sc.
2nd rnd: Ch 2 (does not count as hdc). 1 hdc in same sp as last sl st. 1 hdc in

each of next 5 sc. (2 hdc in next sc) twice. 1 hdc in next sc. (2 hdc in next sc) twice. 1 hdc in each of next 6 sc. 3 hdc in last sc. Join with sl st to first hdc. 24 hdc.

3rd rnd: Ch 1. 1 sc in same sp as last sl st. 1 sc in each of next 6 hdc. (2 hdc in next hdc) 3 times. 3 dc in next hdc (mark center st for toe). (2 hdc in next hdc) 3 times. 1 sc in each of next 8 hdc. 3 sc in next hdc. 1 sc in last hdc. Join with sl st to first sc. 34 sts.

4th rnd: Ch 1. Working in back loops only, 1 sc in same sp as last sl st. 1 sc in each st around. Join with sl st to first sc. Turn.

5th rnd: (WS). Ch 1. Working in back loops only, 1 sc in each sc around. Join with sl st to first sc. Turn.

6th rnd: (RS). Ch 1. Working in back loops only, 1 sc in each sc around. Join with sl st to first sc. Move toe st marker to correct position in last rnd.

7th rnd: Ch 1. 1 sc in same sp as last sl st. 1 sc in each sc until 5 sc before toe st. Sc2tog. 1 sc in next sc. Sc2tog. 1 sc in next sc (toe st). Sc2tog. 1 sc in next sc. Sc2tog. 1 sc in each sc to end of rnd. Join with sl st to first sc. 30 sts.

8th rnd: Ch 1. 1 sc in same sp as last sl st. 1 sc in each sc until 4 sts before toe st. (Sc2tog) twice. 1 sc in next sc (toe st). (Sc2tog) twice. 1 sc in each sc to end of rnd. Join with sl st to first sc. 26 sts.

9th rnd: Ch 1. 1 sc in same sp as last sl st. 1 sc in each sc until 4 sts before toe st. (Sc2tog) twice. 1 sc in next sc (toe st). (Sc2tog) twice. 1 sc in each sc to end of rnd. Join with sl st to first sc. 22 sts.

10th rnd: Ch 1. 1 sc in same sp as last sl st. 1 sc in each st around. Join with sl st to first sc. Fasten off.

Cuff: 1st row: Join yarn with sl st to back loop only of sc after toe st. Ch 1. 1 sc in same sp as last sl st. Working in back loops only, 1 sc in each of next 20 sc. Turn. Leave toe st unworked. (21 sc).

2nd row: (WS). Ch 1. Working in back loops only, 1 sc in each of next 8 sc. (2 sc in next sc. 1 sc in next sc) 3 times. 1 sc in each sc to end of row. Turn. 24 sc.

3rd row: Ch 1. Working in back loops only, 1 sc in each sc to end of row. Turn. Rep last row until Cuff measures 1½" [4 cm]. Fasten off.

POMPOMS (MAKE 2 EACH WITH A AND B)

Wind yarn around 3 fingers approx 50 times. Remove from fingers and tie tightly in center. Cut through each side of loops. Trim to a smooth round shape, approx ¾" [2 cm] diameter. Sew in position securely onto Bootie as shown in photo.

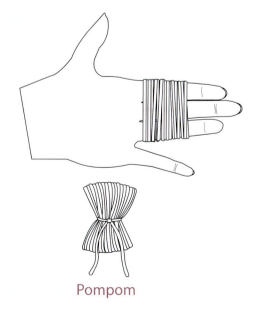

Pompom

ICE CREAM CONE RATTLE

YARN
Bernat® Softee® Baby™ (Solids: 5 oz/140 g; 362 yds/331 m; Ombres: 4.2 oz/120 g; 310 yds/283 m)
Contrast A Little Mouse (30010) 1 ball
Contrast B Mint (02004) or Prettiest Pink (30205) or Lavender Lullaby Ombre (31320) 1 ball

HOOK
Size U.S. E/4 (3.5 mm) crochet hook *or size needed to obtain gauge.*

ADDITIONAL
Small plastic fillable egg
Small amount of dried rice or beans
1 pair of 6 mm plastic safety eyes
Small amount of black embroidery floss for mouth
Embroidery needle

LEARN BY VIDEO
www.go-crafty.com
Ch (chain)
Sc (single crochet)
Slip stitch
Sc2tog (single crochet 2 stitches together)
Dc (double crochet)

MEASUREMENT
Approx 7" [18 cm] tall.

GAUGE
18 sc and 19 rows = 4" [10 cm].

INSTRUCTIONS
CONE
With A, ch 2.
1st rnd: 4 sc in 2nd ch from hook. Join with sl st to first sc.
2nd rnd: Ch 1. 1 sc in each sc around. Join with sl st to first sc.
3rd rnd: Ch 1. 2 sc in each each sc around. Join with sl st to first sc. 8 sc.
4th and 5th rnds: Ch 1. 1 sc in each sc around. Join with sl st to first sc.
6th rnd: Ch 1. 2 sc in first sc. 1 sc in next sc. *2 sc in next sc. 1 sc in next sc. Rep from * around. Join with sl st to first sc. 12 sc.
7th and 8th rnds: As 4th and 5th rnds.
9th rnd: Ch 1. 2 sc in first sc. 1 sc in next sc. *2 sc in next sc. 1 sc in next sc. Rep from * around. Join with sl st to first sc. 18 sc.
10th and 11th rnds: As 4th and 5th rnds.

12th rnd: Ch 1. 2 sc in first sc. 1 sc in each of next 2 sc. *2 sc in next sc. 1 sc in each of next 2 sc. Rep from * around. Join with sl st to first sc. 24 sc.
13th and 14th rnds: As 4th and 5th rnds.
15th rnd: Ch 1. 2 sc in first sc. 1 sc in each of next 3 sc. *2 sc in next sc. 1 sc in each of next 3 sc. Rep from * around. Join with sl st to first sc. 30 sc.
16th and 17th rnds: As 4th and 5th rnds.
18th rnd: Ch 1. 2 sc in first sc. 1 sc in each of next 4 sc. *2 sc in next sc. 1 sc in each of next 4 sc. Rep from * around. Join with sl st to first sc. 36 sc.
19th to 26th rnds: Ch 1. 1 sc in each sc around. Join with sl st to first sc. Fasten off at end of last rnd.
Stuff Cone.

SCOOP
With B, ch 2.
1st rnd: 8 sc in 2nd ch from hook. Join with sl st to first sc.
2nd rnd: Ch 1. 2 sc in each sc around. Join with sl st to first sc. 16 sc.
3rd rnd: Ch 1. 1 sc in each sc around. Join with sl st to first sc.
4th rnd: Ch 1. 2 sc in first sc. 1 sc in next sc. *2 sc in next sc. 1 sc in next sc. Rep from * around. Join with sl st to first sc. 24 sc.
5th rnd: As 3rd rnd.
6th rnd: Ch 1. 2 sc in first sc. 1 sc in each of next 2 sc. *2 sc in next sc. 1 sc in each of next 2 sc. Rep from * around. Join with sl st to first sc. 32 sc.
7th rnd: As 3rd rnd.
8th rnd: Ch 1. 2 sc in first sc. 1 sc in each of next 3 sc. *2 sc in next sc. 1 sc in each of next 3 sc. Rep from * around. Join with sl st to first sc. 40 sc.

9th to 16th rnds: Ch 1. 1 sc in each sc around. Join with sl st to first sc.
17th rnd: Ch 1. *1 sc in each of next 8 sc. Sc2tog. Rep from * around. Join with sl st to first sc. 36 sc.
18th rnd: Ch 1. 1 sc in each st around. Join with sl st to first sc. Do not fasten off.
Attach safety eyes as shown in picture. With black embroidery floss, embroider mouth. Fill plastic egg approx halfway with dried rice or beans. Secure egg opening with tape. Stuff Scoop, inserting egg and stuff around egg.

Join Scoop to Cone: 1st rnd: With bottom edge of Scoop and top edge of Cone aligned, ch 1. Working through both thicknesses, work 1 rnd of sc in each ec around, inserting more stuffing as you go. Join with sl st to first sc.
2nd rnd: Skip first sc. *5 dc in next sc. Skip next sc. Sl st in next sc. Skip next sc. Rep from * around. Join with sl st to first dc.
Fasten off.

CROCHET BABY JACKET SET

YARN
Bernat® Baby Sport™
(12.3 oz/350 g; 1256 yds/1148 m)
Sizes Newborn (3 mos-6/12 mos): Baby Pink (21420)
1 (1-1) ball
Note: 1 ball makes 4 (3-3) Sets.

HOOK
Size U.S. G/6 (4 mm) crochet hook *or size needed to obtain gauge.*

ADDITIONAL
1 button

LEARN BY VIDEO
www.go-crafty.com
Ch (chain)
Dc (double crochet)
Sc (single crochet)
Slip stitch
Hdc (half double crochet)

SIZES
To fit chest measurement
Newborn 14½" [37 cm]
3 mos 16" [40.5 cm]
6/12 mos 17" [43 cm]

Finished chest
Newborn 17" [43 cm]
3 mos 20" [51 cm]
6/12 mos 21" [53.5 cm]

GAUGE
16 dc and 8 rows = 4" [10 cm].

INSTRUCTIONS
The instructions are written for smaller size. If changes are necessary for larger size the instructions will be written thus ( ). When only one number is given, it applies to both sizes.

Notes:
Cardigan is worked in one piece from neck edge down.
Ch 3 at beg of row or rnd counts as dc.

JACKET
Beg at neck edge, ch 46 (54-54).
1st row: (RS). 1 dc in 4th ch from hook. 1 dc in each of next 5 (6-6) ch. (1 dc. Ch 1. 1 dc—V-st made) in next ch. 1 dc in each of next 6 (8-8) ch. V-st in next ch. 1 dc in each of next 14 (16-16) ch. V-st in next ch. 1 dc in each of next 6 (8-8) ch. V-st in next ch. 1 dc in each of last 7 (8-8) ch. Turn.

2nd to 6th (8th-8th) rows: Ch 3. *1 dc in each dc to ch-1 sp of next V-st. V-st in ch-1 sp of next V-st. Rep from * 3 times more. 1 dc in each dc to end of row. Turn. 88 (112-112) dc and 4 ch-1 sps at end of 6th (8th-8th) row.

Divide Sleeves and Body: Next row: (RS). Ch 3. 1 dc in each of next 12 (15-15) dc. 1 dc in ch-1 sp of next V-st. Ch 6 (6-8) for underarm. Skip next 18 (24-24) dc for Sleeve. 1 dc in ch-1 sp of next V-st. 1 dc in each of next 26 (32-32) dc. 1 dc in ch-1 sp of next V-st. Ch 6 (6-8) for underarm. Skip next 18 (24-24) dc for Sleeve. 1 dc in ch-1 sp of next V-st. 1 dc in each of last 13 (16-16) dc. Turn.

Next row: Ch 3. 1 dc in each dc or ch to end of row. Turn. 68(80-84) dc.

Next row: Ch 3. 1 dc in each dc to end of row. Turn.

Rep last row until work from underarm ch measures 5 (5½-6½)" [12.5 (14-16.5) cm].

Fasten off.

Sleeves: 1st rnd: (RS). Join yarn with sl st to center of underarm ch. Ch 3. 1 dc in each ch or dc around. 24 (30-32) dc. Join.

2nd rnd: Ch 3. 1 dc in each dc around. Join.

Rep last rnd until work from underarm ch measures 4½ (5½-6)" [11.5 (14-15) cm].

Fasten off.

Button Band: 1st row: (RS). Join yarn with sl st at corner of Left Front neck edge. Ch 1. Work 1 row of sc evenly down front edge. Turn.

2nd and 3rd rows: Ch 1. 1 sc in each sc to end of row. Turn.

Fasten off.

Buttonhole Band: 1st row: (RS). Join yarn with sl st at lower corner of Right Front edge. Ch 1. Work 1 row of sc evenly up front edge. Turn.

2nd row: Ch 1. 1 sc in first sc. Ch 1. Skip next sc. 1 sc in each sc to end of row. Turn.

3rd row: Ch 1. 1 sc in each sc and ch-1 sp to end of row. Fasten off.

HAT

Note: Ch 2 at beg of rnd does not count as st.

Beg at crown, ch 3.

1st rnd: 8 hdc in 3rd ch from hook. Join with sl st to first hdc.

2nd rnd: Ch 2. 2 hdc in each hdc around. Join with sl st to first hdc. 16 hdc.

3rd rnd: Ch 2. *2 hdc in next hdc. 1 hdc in next hdc. Rep from * around. Join with sl st to first hdc. 24 hdc.

4th rnd: Ch 2. *1 hdc in each of next 2 hdc. 2 hdc in next hdc. Rep from * around. Join with sl st to first hdc. 32 hdc.

5th rnd: Ch 2. *2 hdc in next hdc. 1 hdc in each of next 3 hdc. Rep from * around. Join with sl st to first hdc. 40 hdc.

Size Newborn only: 6th rnd: Ch 2. *2 hdc in next hdc. 1 hdc in each of next 9 hdc. Rep from * around. Join with sl st to first hdc. 44 hdc.

Sizes 3 mos and 6/12 mos only: 6th rnd: Ch 2. *1 hdc in each of next 3 hdc. 2 hdc in next hdc. Rep from * around. Join with sl st to first. 50 hdc.

Size 6/12 mos only: 7th rnd: Ch 2. *2 hdc in next hdc. 1 hdc in each of next 7 hdc. Rep from * to last 2 hdc. 1 hdc in each of last 2 hdc. Join with sl st to first hdc. 56 hdc.

All sizes: Next rnd: Ch 2. 1 hdc in each hdc around. Join with sl st to first hdc. 44 (50-56) hdc.

Rep last rnd until Hat measures approx 4 (4½-5)" [10 (11.5-12.5) cm].

Next rnd: Ch 1. 1 sc in each hdc around. Join with sl st to first sc. Fasten off.

EARS (MAKE 2)

Ch 5 (6-6).

1st rnd: 1 sc in 2nd ch from hook. 1 sc in each of next 2 (3-3) ch. 3 sc in last ch. Working into opposite side of ch, 1 sc in each of next 2 (3-3) ch. 2 sc in last ch. Join with sl st to first sc. 10 (12-12) sc.

2nd rnd: Ch 1. 1 sc in same sp as last sl st. 1 sc in each of next 3 (4-4) sc. 3 sc in next sc. 1 sc in each of next 4 (5-5) sc. 3 sc in last sc. Join with sl st to first sc. 14 (16-16) sc.

3rd rnd: Ch 1. 1 sc in same sp as last sl st. 1 sc in each of next 4 (5-5) sc. 3 sc in next sc. 1 sc in each of next 6 (7-7) sc. 3 sc in next sc. 1 sc in last sc. Join with sl st to first sc. 18 (20-20) sc.

4th to 6th rnds: Ch 1. 1 sc in same sp as last sl st. 1 sc in each sc around. Join with sl st to first sc.

Fasten off, leaving a long end to sew Ear to Hat. Fold Ear flat.

Sew Ears to Hat as shown in photo.

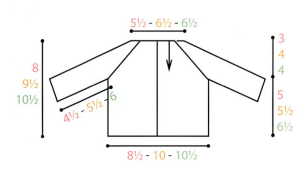

CHECKER CROCHET BABY BLANKET

YARN
Bernat® Baby Blanket Tiny™ (3.5 oz/100 g; 316 yds/288 m)
Contrast A Polar Bear (14003) 2 balls
Contrast B Gray Owl (14002) 2 balls
Contrast C Seedling (14008) 2 balls

HOOK
Size U.S. G/6 (4 mm) crochet hook *or size needed to obtain gauge.*

LEARN BY VIDEO
www.go-crafty.com
Ch (chain)
Dc (double crochet)

SIZE
Approx 40" [101.5 cm] square.

GAUGE
15 sts and 12 rows = 4" [10 cm] in pat.

INSTRUCTIONS
Note: Carry colors when not in use loosely up side of work. To change colors at end of rows, work to last 2 loops on hook of last st in row. Draw new color through last 2 loops and proceed with new color.
With A, ch 155. See chart.

1st row: (WS). 1 dc in 4th ch from hook. *1 dc in next ch. Ch 3. Skip next 3 ch. 1 dc in each of next 3 ch. Rep from * to end of ch. Join B. Turn. 153 sts.

2nd row: With B, ch 3. Skip next 3 dc. *1 dc in each of next 3 ch one row below. Ch 3. Skip next 3 dc. Rep from * ending last rep with skip next 2 dc. 1 sc in top of ch 3. Join C. Turn.

3rd row: With C, ch 3. 1 dc in each of next 2 dc one row below. *Ch 3. Skip next 3 dc. 1 dc in each of next 3 dc one row below. Rep from * to end of row. Join A. Turn.

4th row: With A, ch 3. Skip next 3 dc. *1 dc in each of next 3 dc one row below. Ch 3. Skip next 3 dc. Rep from * ending last rep with skip next 2 dc. 1 sc in top of ch 3. Join B. Turn.

5th row: With B, ch 3. 1 dc in each of next 2 dc one row below. *Ch 3. Skip next 3 dc. 1 dc in each of next 3 dc one row below. Rep from * to end of row. Join C. Turn.

6th row: With C, ch 3. Skip next 3 dc. *1 dc in each of next 3 dc one row below. Ch 3. Skip next 3 dc. Rep from * ending last rep with skip next 2 dc. 1 sc in top of ch 3. Join A. Turn.

7th row: With A, ch 3. 1 dc in each of next 2 dc one row below. *Ch 3. Skip next 3 dc. 1 dc in each of next 3 dc one row below. Rep from * to end of row. Join B.

8th row: With B, ch 3. Skip next 3 dc. *1 dc in each of next 3 dc one row below. Ch 3. Skip next 3 dc. Rep from * ending last rep with skip next 2 dc. 1 sc in top of ch 3. Join C. Turn.

Rep 3rd to 8th rows for pat until work measures approx 40" [101.5 cm] from beg, ending on a 7th row of pat. Fasten off.

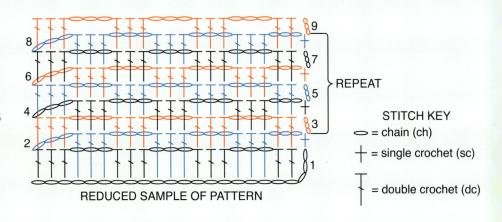

REDUCED SAMPLE OF PATTERN

STITCH KEY
◯ = chain (ch)
+ = single crochet (sc)
† = double crochet (dc)

TAKING SIDES CROCHET CARDIGAN

YARN
Bernat® Baby Blanket Tiny™
(3.5 oz/100 g; 316 yds/288 m)
Size 6 (12) mos: Seedling (14008)
1 (2) ball(s)

HOOK
Size U.S. H/8 (5 mm)
crochet hook *or size needed
to obtain gauge.*

ADDITIONAL
Stitch markers
1 button

LEARN BY VIDEO
www.go-crafty.com
Ch (chain)
Sc (single crochet)
Slip stitch

SIZES
To fit chest measurement
6 mos 17" [43 cm]
12 mos 18" [45.5 cm])

GAUGE
16 sts and 13 rows = 4" [10 cm] in pat.

INSTRUCTIONS
The instructions are written for smaller size. If changes are necessary for larger size the instructions will be written thus ( ).
Note: Body is worked in one piece to armholes.

BODY
Chain (Ch) 86 (92).
**1st row: [Right Side (RS)]. 1 single crochet (sc) in 2nd ch from hook. *Ch 1. Skip next ch. 1 sc in next ch. Repeat

(Rep) from * to end of chain. Turn. 85 (91) stitches (sts).

2nd row: Ch 1. 1 sc in first sc. *1 sc in next ch-1 space (sp). Ch 1. Skip next sc. Rep from * to last 2 sts. 1 sc in next ch-1 sp. 1 sc in last sc. Turn.

3rd row: Ch 1. 1 sc in first sc. *Ch 1. Skip next sc. 1 sc in next ch-1 sp. Rep from * to last 2 sts. Ch 1. Skip next sc. 1 sc in last sc. Turn.**
Rep 2nd and 3rd rows for pattern (pat) until 7" [18 cm] total length, ending on a Wrong Side (WS) row.

Divide for armholes: Right Front:
1st row: (RS). Pat across 19 (21) sts. Turn. Leave remaining (rem) sts unworked.
Continue (Cont) even in pat on 19 (21) sts for 12 (14) more rows. Fasten off.

Back: With RS facing, join yarn with slip stitch (sl st) in next st. Beginning (Beg) in same sp as last sl st, pat across next 39 (41) sts. Turn. Leave rem sts unworked.
Cont even in pat on 39 (41) sts for 12 (14) more rows. Fasten off.

Left Front: With RS facing, join yarn with sl st in next st. Beg in same sp as last sl st, pat across next 27 (29) sts. Turn.
Cont even in pat on 27 (29) sts for 12 (14) more rows. Fasten off.

SLEEVES

Ch 34 (38). Work from ** to ** as given for Body. 33 (37) sts.
Rep 2nd and 3rd rows for pat until 7½ (8½)" [19 (21.5) cm] total length, ending on a WS row. Fasten off.

FINISHING

Place markers along final row of Fronts and Back 10 (11) sts in from armhole edges for shoulders. Sew shoulder seams to markers.

Collar: 1st row: [Wrong Side (WS)]. Join yarn with sl st in corner of Left Front at neck edge. Ch 1. Beg in same sp as last sl st, pat across 17 (18) sts of Left Front neck edge, 19 sts across back neck edge and 9 (10) sts across Right Front neck edge. Turn. 45 (47) sts. Work 2¼" [5.5 cm] in pat. Fasten off.

Sew in Sleeves. Sew sleeve seams. Place garment on flat surface. Lap Left over Right Front and place button marker on Right Front 4½" [11.5 cm] down from top edge of Collar and 2" [5 cm] in from front edge. Stitch around openwork sp in pat to create buttonhole on Left Front to correspond to marker.
Sew on button to correspond to buttonhole.

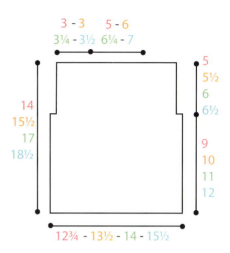

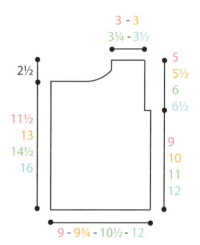

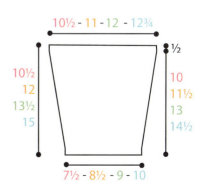

ELFIN CROCHET CARDIGAN

YARN
Bernat® Baby Blanket Tiny™
(3.5 oz/100 g; 316 yds/288 m)
Size 6 (12) mos:
Contrast A Sunflower (14007)
2 (2) balls
Contrast B Gray Owl (14002)
1 (1) ball

HOOK
Size U.S. 7 (4.5 mm) crochet hook
or size needed to obtain gauge.

ADDITIONAL
Stitch markers
3 buttons
Stuffing for pompom

LEARN BY VIDEO
www.go-crafty.com
Ch (chain)
Sc (single crochet)
Dc (double crochet)
Slip stitch

SIZES
To fit chest measurement
6 mos 17" [43 cm]
12 mos 18" [45.5 cm]

Finished chest measurement
19½" [49.5 cm]
21½" [54.5 cm]

GAUGE
14 sts and 12 rows = 4" [10 cm] in pat.

18

INSTRUCTIONS

The instructions are written for smaller size. If changes are necessary for larger size the instructions will be written thus ( ).

Note: Body is worked in one piece. Ch 3 at beg of row counts as dc.

BODY

With A, ch 72 (78).
**1st row: (RS). 1 sc in 2nd ch from hook. *1 dc in next ch. 1 sc in next ch. Rep from * to end of chain. Turn. 71 (77) sts.
2nd row: Ch 3. *1 sc in next dc. 1 dc in next sc. Rep from * to end of row. Turn.
3rd row: Ch 1. 1 sc in first dc. *1 dc in next sc. 1 sc in next dc. Rep from * to end of row. Turn. ** Rep last 2 rows for pat until 7" [18 cm] total length, ending on a WS row.

Divide for armholes: Right Front: 1st row: (RS). Ch 1. Pat across 15 (17) sts. Turn. Leave rem sts unworked. Cont even in pat on 15 (17) sts for 12 (14) more rows.
Fasten off.

Back: With RS facing, skip next 7 sts. Join yarn with sl st in next st. Ch 1 and pat across next 27 (29) sts. Turn. Leave rem sts unworked.
Cont even in pat on 27 (29) sts for 12 (14) more rows. Fasten off.

Left Front: With RS facing, skip next 7 sts. Join yarn with sl st in next st. Ch 1 and pat across next 15 (17) sts. Turn. Cont even in pat on 15 (17) sts for 12 (14) more rows. Fasten off. PM along final row of Fronts and Back 6 (7) sts in from armhole edges for shoulders. Sew shoulder seams.

SLEEVES

With A, ch 30 (34). Work from ** to ** as given for Body. 29 (33) sts. Work in pat until 7½ (8½)" [19 (21.5) cm] total length, ending on a WS row. Fasten off. PM on side edges 1" [2.5 cm] down from final row.

HOOD

Beg at face edge, with A, ch 54 (58). Work from ** to ** as given for Body. 53 (57) sts. Work in pat until 6 (6½)" [15 (16.5) cm] total length, ending on a WS row. Fasten off.

Fold last row in half and sew center back seam. Sew sides of Hood to neck edge (easing in Hood as needed).

FINISHING

With RS facing, PM for 3 buttonholes on Right Front: top hole ½" [1 cm] below neck edge, bottom hole 7" [18 cm] above lower edge and rem hole centered between. St around openwork sp in pat for buttonholes ¾" [2 cm] from front edge. Sew on buttons to correspond to buttonholes. Sew in Sleeves, placing rows above markers along unworked sts at armholes to form square armholes.

POMPOM

With B, ch 12. Work from ** to ** as given for Body. 11 sts. Work in pat until 3" [7.5 cm] total length. Fasten off, leaving a long end. Thread end onto tapestry needle and gather around outer edges of Pompom, inserting stuffing before fastening off. Sew to point of Hood.

PURRRFECT CROCHET PLAY RUG

YARN
Bernat® Baby Blanket™ (10.5 oz/300 g; 220 yds/201 m)
Main Color (MC) Baby Sand (04010) 4 balls (780 yds/713 m)

Bernat® Baby Blanket™ (3.5 oz/100 g; 72 yds/65 m)
Contrast A Vanilla (03008) 1 ball (50 yds/46 m)
Contrast B Baby Pink (03200) 1 ball (35 yds/32 m)

HOOK
Sizes U.S. N/15 (10 mm) and U.S. L/11 (8 mm) crochet hooks *or size needed to obtain gauge.*

LEARN BY VIDEO
www.go-crafty.com
Ch (chain)
Dc (double crochet)
Slip stitch
Sc (single crochet)
Sc2tog (single crochet 2 stitches together)
Sc3tog (single crochet 3 stitches together)

MEASUREMENT
Approx 35" [89 cm] in diameter.

GAUGE
6 dc and 4 rows = 4" [10 cm] with larger hook and yarn held double.

INSTRUCTIONS
Note: Ch 3 at beg of rnd counts as dc.

FACE
With 2 strands of MC held tog and larger hook, ch 4. Join with sl st to first ch to form ring.
1st rnd: Ch 3. 11 dc in ring. Join with wl st to top of ch 3. 12 dc.
2nd rnd: Ch 3. 1 dc in first dc. 2 dc in each dc around. Join with sl st to top of ch 3. 24 dc.
3rd rnd: Ch 3. 1 dc in first dc. 1 dc in next dc. *2 dc in next dc. 1 dc in next dc. Rep from * around. Join with sl st to top of ch 3. 36 dc.
4th rnd: Ch 3. 1 dc in first dc. 1 dc in each of next 2 dc. *2 dc in next dc. 1 dc in each of next 2 dc. Rep from * around. Join with sl st to top of ch 3. 48 dc.
5th rnd: Ch 3. 1 dc in first dc. 1 dc in each of next 3 dc. *2 dc in next dc. 1 dc in each of next 3 dc. Rep from * around. Join with sl st to top of ch 3. 60 dc.
6th rnd: Ch 3. 1 dc in first dc. 1 dc in each of next 4 dc. *2 dc in next dc. 1 dc in each of next 4 dc. Rep from * around. Join with sl st to top of ch 3. 72 dc.
7th rnd: Ch 3. 1 dc in first dc. 1 dc in each of next 5 dc. *2 dc in next dc. 1 dc in each of next 5 dc. Rep from * around. Join with sl st to top of ch 3. 84 dc.
8th rnd: Ch 3. 1 dc in first dc. 1 dc in each of next 6 dc. *2 dc in next dc. 1 dc in each of next 6 dc. Rep from * around. Join with sl st to top of ch 3. 96 dc.
9th rnd: Ch 3. 1 dc in first dc. 1 dc in each of next 7 dc. *2 dc in next dc. 1 dc in each of next 7 dc. Rep from * around. Join with sl st to top of ch 3. 108 dc.
Cont as established, inc 12 dc every rnd until piece measures approx. 35" [89 cm] in diameter. Fasten off.

EARS (MAKE 2)
With 2 strands of MC held tog and larger hook, ch 18.
1st row: 1 sc in 2nd ch from hook. 1 sc in each ch to end of chain. Turn. 17 sc.
2nd row: Ch 1. 1 sc in each sc to end of row. Turn.
3rd row: Ch 1. Sc2tog. 1 sc in each sc to last 2 sc. Sc2tog. Turn. 15 sts.
4th row: Ch 1. 1 sc in each st to end of row. Turn.
Rep last 2 rows to 3 sts.
Next row: Ch 1. Sc3tog. Fasten off.

INNER EAR (MAKE 2)
With 1 strand of B and smaller hook, ch 14.
1st row: 1 sc in 2nd ch from hook. 1 sc in each ch to end of chain. Turn. 13 sc.
2nd row: Ch 1. Sc2tog. 1 sc in each sc to last 2 sc. Sc2tog. 11 sts.
3rd row: Ch 1. 1 sc in each st to end of row. Turn.
Rep last 2 rows to 3 sts.
Next row: Ch 1. Sc3tog. Fasten off.
Sew Inner Ear to Ear as shown in picture.

EYES (MAKE 2)
With 1 strand of A and smaller hook, ch 4.
1st rnd: 9 dc in 4th ch from hook. Join with sl st to top of ch 3. 10 dc. 2nd rnd: Ch 3 (counts as dc). 1 dc in first dc (counts as 2 dc). 2 dc in each dc around. Join with sl st to top of ch 3. 20 dc.

3rd rnd: Ch 3 (counts as dc). 1 dc in first dc (counts as 2 dc). 1 dc in next dc. *2 dc in next dc. 1 dc in next dc. Rep from * around. Join with sl st to top of ch 3. 30 dc. Fasten off.

PUPIL (MAKE 2)
With 1 strand of MC and smaller hook, ch 4.
Work from ** to ** as given for Eye. Fasten off.

Sew Pupil to Eye as shown in picture.

NOSE
With 1 strand of B and smaller hook, ch 9.
1st row: (RS). 1 sc in 2nd ch from hook. 1 sc in each ch to end of chain. Turn. 8 sc.
2nd row: Ch 1. Sc2tog. 1 sc in each sc to last 2 sc. Sc2tog. Turn. 6 sts.
3rd row: As 2nd row. 4 sts.
4th row: Ch 1. (Sc2tog) twice. 2 sts.
5th row: Ch 1. Sc2tog. Do not fasten off.
Ch 1. Work 1 rnd of sc around 3 edges, working 3 sc in each corner.
Join with sl st to first sc. Fasten off.

FINISHING
Sew Eyes, Nose and Ears to Face as shown in picture.

MOUTH
With 2 strands of A and smaller hook, ch 30. Fasten off.
With 2 strands of A and smaller hook, ch 15. Fasten off.
Sew longer chain to Face, starting at tip of Nose and curving up to form Mouth. Sew shorter chain to form other side of Mouth.

WHISKERS (MAKE 4)
With 2 strands of A and smaller hook, ch 12. Fasten off.
Sew 2 Whiskers on either side of face as shown in picture.

LITTLE DREAMWEAVER BLANKET

YARN
Bernat® Baby Blanket™
(10.5 oz/300 g; 220 yds/201 m)
Main Color (MC) Little Sandcastles (04011) 2 balls or 422 yds/386 m
Contrast A Baby Teal (04734) 1 ball or 142 yds/130 m

HOOK
Size U.S. N/15 (10 mm) crochet hook *or size needed to obtain gauge.*

ADDITIONAL
Large blunt-tip needle (for weaving)

LEARN BY VIDEO
www.go-crafty.com
Ch (chain)
Sc (single crochet)
Slip stitch

MEASUREMENT
Approx 38" [96.5 cm] square.

GAUGE
5 sc and 6 rows = 4" [10 cm].

INSTRUCTIONS
With MC, chain (ch) 64.
1st row: 1 single crochet (sc) in 2nd ch from hook. *Ch 1. Skip next ch. 1 sc in next ch. Repeat (rep) from * to end of chain. Turn. 55 stitches (sts).
2nd row: Ch 1. 1 sc in first sc. 1 sc in next ch-1 space (sp). *Ch 1. Skip next sc. 1 sc in next ch-1 sp. Rep from * to last sc. 1 sc in last sc. Turn.
3rd row: Ch 1. 1 sc in first sc. *Ch 1. Skip next sc. 1 sc in next ch-1 sp. Rep from * to last 2 sc. Ch 1. Skip next sc. 1 sc in last sc. Turn.
Rep 2nd and 3rd rows until work from beginning (beg) measures 34" [86.5 cm]. Fasten off.

WOVEN STRIPES
Note: Weave with the longest strand that is comfortable to avoid having a large number of ends.
Thread a long strand of A through blunt-tip needle, having yarn doubled. Beg at right side edge of 2nd row, weave yarn in and out through ch-1 sps to left side edge. Rep weaving through every 4th row, using the same strand of yarn where possible and carrying yarn up side of work.

BORDER
1st round (rnd): Join A with slip stitch (sl st) to any corner. Ch 1. Work 53 sc evenly across each side of Blanket, working 3 sc in each corner and working around ends left from weaving. Join with sl st in first sc.
2nd and 3rd rnds: Ch 1. 1 sc in each sc around, working 3 sc in each corner sc. Join with sl st to first sc. Fasten off. ■

MOUSIE SNOOD

YARN
Bernat® Baby Blanket™
(3.5 oz/100 g; 72 yds/65 m)
Sizes 12/18 mos (2/4 yrs): Main
Color (MC) Sand Baby (03010)
2 (3) balls
Contrast A Baby Pink (03200)
1 (1) ball

HOOK
Size U.S. L/11 (8 mm)
crochet hook *or size needed
to obtain gauge.*

LEARN BY VIDEO
www.go-crafty.com
Ch (chain)
Hdc (half double crochet)
Sc (single crochet)
Slip stitch

SIZES
To fit sizes 12/18 mos (2/4 yrs)
Approx 13 (15)" [33 (38) cm] around x
11 (13)" [28 (33) cm] deep.

GAUGE
7 sc and 8 rows = 4" [10 cm]

INSTRUCTIONS
The instructions are written for smaller size. If changes are necessary for larger size the instructions will be written thus ( ). When only one number is given, it applies to both sizes. For ease in working, circle all numbers pertaining to your size.
Note: Snood begins at face edge. With MC, ch 34 (38). Join in ring with sl st to first ch, being careful to not twist chain.

1st rnd: Ch 2 (does not count as st). 1 hdc in each ch around. Join with sl st to first hdc. 34 (38) hdc.
2nd rnd: Ch 1. 1 sc in each of next 4 hdc. 1 hdc in each of next 4 hdc. 1 dc in each of next 18 (22) hdc. 1 hdc in each of next 4 hdc. 1 sc in each of last 4 hdc. Join with sl st to first sc.
3rd rnd: Ch 1. 1 sc in each of first 4 sc. 1 hdc in each of next 4 hdc. 1 dc in each of next 18 (22) dc. 1 hdc in each of next 4 hdc. 1 sc in each of last 4 sc. Join with sl st to first sc.
Rep last rnd until work from beg down longer side measures 11 (13)" [28 (33) cm]. Fasten off.

EARS
OUTER EAR (MAKE 2)
With MC, ch 3.
1st rnd: 8 hdc in 3rd ch from hook. Join with sl st to first hdc. Fasten off.

INNER EAR (MAKE 2)
With A, ch 3.
1st rnd: 8 hdc in 3rd ch from hook. Join with sl st to first hdc. Fasten off.

With WS of Outer and Inner Ears tog and with Inner Ear facing, join MC with sl st to any sc.
1st rnd: Working through both thicknesses, ch 1 and work sc evenly around outer edge of Ears. Join with sl st to first sc.
Fasten off.

Sew Ears in position as shown in photo.

SIMPLE CROCHET BABY PONCHO

YARN
Bernat® Baby Blanket Tiny™ (3.5 oz/100 g; 316 yds/288 m)
Sizes 6/12 (18/24) mos:
Wildflowers (14011) 1 (2) ball(s)

HOOK
Size U.S. 7 (4.5 mm) crochet hook *or size needed to obtain gauge.*

ADDITIONAL
Stitch marker

LEARN BY VIDEO
www.go-crafty.com
Ch (chain)
Sc (single crochet)
Dc (double crochet)

SIZES
To fit chest measurement
6/12 mos 17–18" [43-45.5 cm]
18/24 mos 19–20" [48-51 cm]

GAUGE
14 sts and 10 rows = 4" [10 cm] in pattern.

INSTRUCTIONS
The instructions are written for smaller size. If changes are necessary for larger sizes the instructions will be written thus ( ). When only one number is given, it applies to all sizes.
Chain (ch) 62 (66).
1st row: (Right side—RS). 1 single crochet (sc) in 4th ch from hook (skipped ch-3 counts as double crochet—dc). *1 dc in next ch. 1 sc in next ch. Repeat (rep) from * to end of row. Turn. 60 (64) stitches (sts).
2nd row: Ch 3 (counts as dc). 1 sc in next dc. *1 dc in next sc. 1 sc in next dc. Rep from * to end of row. Turn. Rep last row for pattern (pat) until work from beginning (beg) measures approximately (approx) 9 (10)" [23 (25.5) cm], ending on a wrong side (WS) row.
Next row: Pat across first 32 (36) sts. Turn. Leave remaining (rem) sts unworked. Place marker at end of row. Continue (cont) in pat on these 32 (36) sts until work from marker measures approx 17" [43 cm], ending on a wrong side WS row.
Fasten off.

Place marker on left edge of work 9 (10)" [23 (25.5) cm] down from last row. Fold work, sewing together (tog) as seen in diagram.

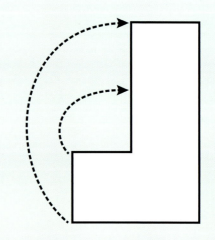